A Small Girl's 1960s Launceston

Diana Reynolds

A Small Girl's 1960s Launceston

Diana Reynolds

On the old Springfield property where some of my Dad's family came from, wild daffodils grew.

For my mother Mary Reynolds -
an inspiring wunderkind for us all.

Foreword

Like the author, Diana Reynolds, I spent much of my childhood on the Trevallyn hillside in Launceston, Tasmania. It was a wonderful open suburb for youngsters growing up in the 1950's where parents could assume children were safe to explore the bush and nearby Cataract Gorge Cliffgrounds. Most weekends and school holidays I headed off in the early morning with my friends to enjoy a day of imaginative play and adventure. We took our sandwiches in brown paper bags and disappeared from parental direction to amuse ourselves until teatime.

There was usually an older 'leader of the gang' who kept a watchful eye on younger members and made decisions for all of us. We survived this very happy period of freedom despite the inevitable scratches, cuts and bruises. We also learned some skills in cooperation and self reliance taking risks as we negotiated steep slopes and avoided the occasional snake.

Diana Reynolds' book reminds me of those carefree days even though she grew up more than twenty years later. Her stories and images are so familiar that I can relive the excitement of Regatta Night fireworks or crossing the swinging bridge as winter storm waters roared below tumbling into First Basin and down the Gorge. I played in the same school playground and rode in a billy cart down the same hill. I even spent time in the same hospital when my tonsils were removed!

Diana's detailed pictures are a delight about a world that has changed but one that can be revisited today. We can still explore the bush and the beach to interact with our natural environment. City Park has its monkeys and the Cliffgrounds its peacocks.

Both old timers like me and a new generation will be charmed by this book and will well understand why it is called 'A Small Girl's 1960's Launceston.'

Margaret Reynolds

Margaret Reynolds was born in Launceston in 1941 and attended Trevallyn Primary and Launceston High schools. She trained as a teacher at the University of Tasmania, teaching on the North West Coast and New Norfolk before travelling overseas and then settling in North Queensland. She was senator and minister in the Australian Parliament 1983 - 1999 before returning to live in Launceston until 2011 when she moved south to Richmond.

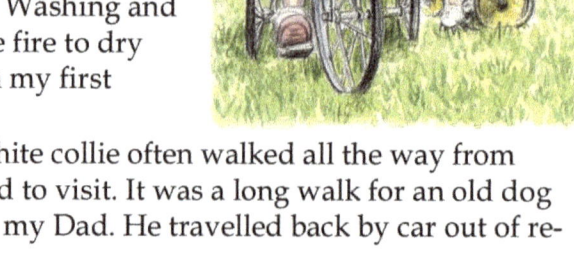

As a new baby I came home to a new house my parents had actually built themselves high up on the top of West Launceston. Hardwicke Street, Summerhill seemed to be way out in the country back then - unsealed roads, no bus service and no telephone. The house was typical of the 1950's with innovative features such as unusual angles and bright colours. The chimney dominated the front - inside and outside were clad in crazy-paving sandstone. My dad designed the house. At the time he was working as a Window Dresser and had quite a flair for design.

The fireplace was the single source of heating, so life in the cold Launceston winters was spent in front of the fire. Washing and nappies were hung above the fire to dry and consequently featured in my first drawing as a child.

Nero, Dad's old black and white collie often walked all the way from Nanna's house in Talbot Road to visit. It was a long walk for an old dog who was missing his master, my Dad. He travelled back by car out of respect for his age.

Summers were such fun. In our large backyard we had a really big swing and a plastic - very new! - paddling pool. It was very popular with everyone. Roslyn and I played on our trikes while Marcus learnt to crawl then toddle about. However, within a few years Mum and Dad had decided to sell this house and build us a new home at Trevallyn.

Sometimes we went to visit Mum's friend Margaret Carrington and her little girls who lived beside the South Esk at Hadspen. It was a large property with an orchard of hazelnuts running down to the water. The front gate was set in a tall thick hedge. On the way to the old homestead we passed a large lily pond ringed with flat sandstones. On every stone sat bright green shiny frogs.
Mum said to Marcus and I, 'look at the horrid fake frogs,' and we walked on.
I turned back to take another look.
'Mummy, the froggies are all gone!'
The frogs were real after all. They were actually a native Tasmanian species, the Green and Gold Frog.

Froggy accessories such as hair clips and brooches were popular for little girls back then. Clicker frogs that jumped were lots of fun. As a special treat we loved to eat Freddo frogs when out shopping with Mum.

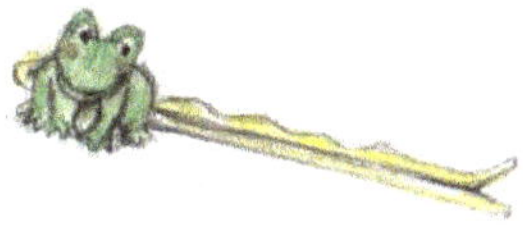

Living in Launceston meant we had all the advantages of a vibrant town but could easily get out to the country in a matter of minutes. Often we would stop at signs posted along country roads for fresh produce – eggs or veggies or fruits in season. Sometimes it was just an honesty box arrangement for collecting the goods and paying for them, usually in a small weathered open shed, where the milk would have once been collected from the farm. At other times we drove right into the farm itself and Mum or Dad might have a chat with the owners while we kids would get out of the car and run about in excitement.

We were sometimes fortunate enough to find a farmer willing to sell us fresh milk. Mum and Dad carried two big silver billies and a Tupperware jug or two in the car and we'd time it to arrive just at milking time. During the drive we'd see the milk laden cows following each other across the paddocks to the milking shed. Often Dad would have to slow the car down to a standstill to let a herd of dairy cows pass across the road to go and get milked. Herds of sheep also were a regular car stopper. Sometimes we'd be allowed to watch the cows being milked. We kids thought the nozzles they put on the cow's teats hilarious and found the whole milking process was extremely busy and fascinating. Best of all we sometimes got a ladleful of warm fresh milk straight from the cows.

The Sunday drive was a regular weekly event and with so many marvellous places a stone's throw from Launceston, we were spoiled for choice. Mum packed up a wicker basket with sandwiches and a Tupperware jug of blackcurrant cordial and by mid morning we were in the land of adventuring. After our picnic and the regulation wait for food to go down to stop 'stitches', we could explore where ever we were visiting.

At Corralyn, there was a partial island for us to have adventures on while parents picnicked on the bank. Little towns like Evandale, Perth and Longford were also favourite destinations. Driving out to Entally House or Clarendon House, or just spotting old abandoned houses to investigate was also fun. Sometimes Dad had the boat in town, so we'd go out on the Tamar River for a spin or to take Mum and friends out waterskiing.

Another attraction to living in Trevallyn was that my Dad's brother Geoff lived there already with his wife Pat, across the way in Cosgrove Street.

Sometimes we would visit them but they had decided early not to have children. This meant there wasn't a lot for three children to do there as there were no swing sets or toys to play with and we were warned to be careful with their things. We did enjoy visiting them though because they had a funny little terrier dog called Bottomly, named so because his bottom wobbled. Hilarious! At a time where everyone had children it did seem a touch perplexing to Roslyn and I that they hadn't any and loved their dog as much as other families loved their children. Of course we didn't dwell on such conundrums and loved them anyway, especially Pat who seemed very glamorous.

Geoff worked at Jessups, a big electrical shop in town, eventually becoming Assistant Manager there. Pat worked at D.W. Murray and Ludbrooks, where she became Assistant Director. Jessups was an upcoming business with lots of gleaming goods and gadgets– a magnet for mums and dads like mine who wanted new appliances to make our lives easier.

Later Roslyn stayed with Pat and Geoff one summer when she worked at the Cataract Gorge Tearooms instead of going to Bridport for our annual holidays.

One day in the Summer holidays Dad took us to spend the day at East Beach, Low Head. It was a working day for Dad doing AMP work at Georgetown.
We were still waiting for Dad to come and get us when the sky began to colour up with sunset. I remember wandering off by myself along the beach when I saw a dark shape in the distance. I was astonished to see a huge wet seal lounging at the water's edge.
'Muummmy! I ran back along the beach to tell everyone. Excitedly we all went to look at the seal while it gazed back at us, wet and impervious. How could I forget such a wonder?

The beach at Badger's Head, on the western side of the Tamar had heaps of flotsam and jetsam piled high along the tide line. We always went with another family in case we got caught by the tide, so far from help. The west wind had left the remnants of many lost ships and yachts which the Daddies made platforms to park the cars on. We also found Aboriginal flints in the many middens and sometimes saw fairy penguins and mutton birds.

Bennett's Wallaby

Pink Galahs

Tasmanian Devil

Pied Currawong

Short Beaked Echidna

Tasmanian Wombat

Eastern Barred Bandicoot

Blue Tongued Lizard

Australian birds and animals are often quite fearless around humans. One day a big kangaroo bounded in through our front gate and jumped down the back to the bush sanctuary. One evening a currawong flew into the kitchen and sat on the towel rack. It gazed about for a few minutes before calmly hopping back out the window. Often Dad would slow down in the car to let an echidna cross the road and we'd watch it digging itself into the earth nearby. Wombats grazing were another lovely sight at dusk. We never actually saw a devil in the wild, but sometimes heard their growling. At Launceston and Bridport bandicoots dug holes and grazed in the garden. Some kids kept Blue Tongue Lizards as pets though it was illegal to do so. The biggest surprise was to find huge Emperor Gum moths beating on the big front windows at our shack at Bridport.

Sometimes we visited our Turner grandparents. Dad-dad Turner had a wonderful old grey timber shed where, when younger, he made furniture. He had worked as a carpenter and cabinet-maker. Arthritis had made him seem very old to us children, especially when we wanted to explore his shed. There were all sorts of very old tools hanging up neatly on pegboard, jars with all sorts of nuts, bolts, screws and nails. There were lots of old magazines and dusty cardboard boxes begging to be explored. I would have loved to fossick in amongst all those treasures! Even after he died, Nanna kept the shed locked.

The backyard at Nanna's had an extensive vegetable garden with every plant in neat rows. Sometimes the grandparents bought heaps of carrots and silver beet for us. It was a most productive patch. Nanna had her flower garden in the front garden. It was beautifully laid out with rows of white Nerine lilies and Hyacinths. She was on the church committee at St. Marks Church and dressed the church with her flowers for all important occasions. Her flowers were very much appreciated.

I'll never forget picking raspberries over at Nannas. It was one for the billy and one for me. The old dog Nero had perfected the art of neatly picking raspberries for himself and we were surprised to see our dog Sandy doing the same trick. Sandy could not have learnt it from Nero as he grew up after the old dog. Perhaps it is a skill embedded in collective doggie memory.

The chook-house was a huge feature up at the top of the garden. Dozens of white Leghorn chooks glared at us with their beady red eyes. I recall being quite frightened of them. We could take grain from a hessian sack and feed the chooks while gathering the eggs.

Sometimes we could take eggs home with us in a brown paper bag. Mum would make the loveliest cakes with them, showing us the double yolked eggs when she cracked them into the bowl.

Nanna's old Singer sewing machine stood on the back porch. I don't remember her using it very often - only to turn collars on Granddad's shirts. My sister Roslyn and I spent many a cold winter's day at Nanna's place. As older girls we turned the sewing machine up onto the Singer sewing bench and learnt the rhythm of pushing the iron foot plate to sew.
Nanna also taught us to make small tapestries and tried to interest us in her favourite skill - making fine doilies with a crochet hook. Framed above her piano was one of my favourites: a beautiful lace butterfly.

Nanna was from a very thrifty generation. She saved chocolate from Christmas to Easter and we children were astonished to receive chocolate that was white with age.

A visit to City Park has always been a place favourite for mothers and small children. The Macaque monkeys were housed then in very cheerless accommodation. They entertained everyone with their antics, particularly when the babies were on show. I'll never forget gazing with horror at their terribly sore-looking red bottoms. A trip to the park sometimes meant a small bag of peanuts for the monkeys and another of old crusts for the solitary white swan who once bit Marcus on his little finger! A little train drove children around the park while in the playground. There was an old steam locomotive for kids to play on which was a great hit. The locomotive was eventually retired to the Don River Railway and replaced with a modern play-gym train.

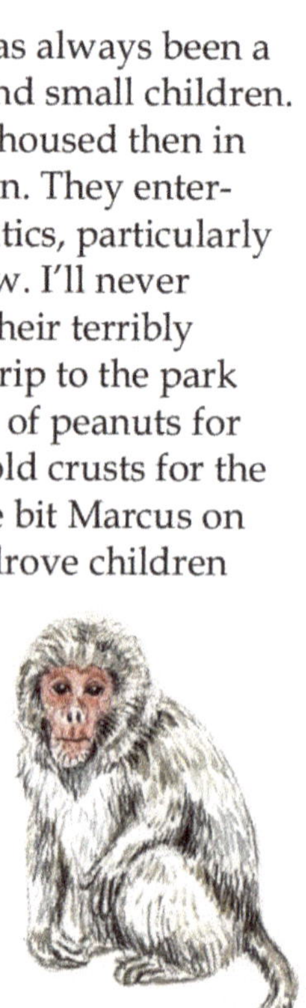

During the week before the long weekend in February 1964, Dad came home from work telling us excitedly about the open-wheel single-seater racing cars he'd seen on trailers about Launceston, as contestants came off the ferry from interstate. They were here for the Tasman series – a new 14 mile (23 km) race on the Longford Circuit, the site for the fastest motor racing in the southern Hemisphere, he told us. We were very impressed to hear drivers could get up to 180 miles (289 km) per hour, but didn't understand how fast that was until we saw it.

Dad was a big fan of Jack Brabham, so in 1964 we took a picnic and went to see the last race of the day– the third Pacific Gold Star Championship between Brabham and 15 other aspirants. Marcus, Roslyn and I were surprised to see tents and Mum said people camped out, waiting for the big event. We found a park out in a paddock with all the other cars and made our way to the busy grandstands. Dad wanted to get closer, so Marcus being a four year old tiddler, got a ride on Dad's shoulders while Roslyn and I stood on prickly hay bales on a spectator mound. We thought it funny to see people standing on the bonnets of their cars to watch. Everyone was terribly excited and we watched a race with big holdens and other touring cars and Tasmanian drivers first.

The noise! My little ears went into shock, but Mum had bought some cotton wool to stuff in our ears so that helped. How could big men fit into those tiny cars I wondered? Daddy and Marcus were having a marvellous time and when the big race began with a wave of the Australian flag, we all walked out to near the viaduct to watch the cars tear along underneath, all blurs of speed, noise and colour. Late in the race Brabham got knocked out because his engine stopped working, my Daddy yelled to us.

We all cheered when the race was won by a great British racing driver, Graham Hill.

My Mum's first car was a green Morris Minor. This was replaced by a tiny white Fiat Bambini. We kids were driven all over Launceston and the surrounding country for picnics and visits in this little car.

Unfortunately the Fiat met with an accident. While driving down Bathurst Street, a truck backed out of a narrow lane. The driver did not see our tiny car with rear view sight limited by the lane and his load. Mum had just bought a lovely new dinner-set with tiger lilies on it from Cox Brothers. The lorry's tray swiped the bonnet off the Fiat before it stopped. We were very shocked!

For months afterwards, until we had a new bonnet fitted, I felt embarrassed and would hide in the back seat when we went out in the Fiat. Being very young, I thought that the bonnet was similar to underpants and the as front of the car was all exposed it was very rude and people would be horrified at the car exposing itself.

My Dad loved his cars almost as much as he loved our boat. When Mum and Dad were young Dad drove a pink Consul – it was the car I came home in when I was born.
Dad felt it was important to make the right impression when he began working at the AMP, so there was a yearly procession of new vehicles after I was four.
A green and white Ford Falcon station-wagon was great for the kids and holidays but became fatigued after a year of towing our heavy boat. Next year a brown Falcon station-wagon suffered the same fate. Dad switched to a maroon Fairlane sedan followed by a black one. Both proved too hot for the Tasmanian summer! We had a white Fairlane the next year until Dad switched to a Toyota Corona.

My little brother Marcus naturally took a great interest in cars. He had a collection of car cards in a Golden Fleece album. Matchbox cars and trucks littered the floor of his bedroom and later he received an impressive poster of a XR falcon that he loved.

Tasmanians are quite used to 'five seasons in one day' and we were no different; unless it was really extreme weather, we regularly went on weekend drives around Launceston or further afield. In summer it was lovely to go for a drive, but with no safety lock on back windows, parents were often concerned about children falling out. In the back, we had to be satisfied with a small side window for a breeze and often fought for the window spot.

In winter, even a drive to school meant parents boiling the kettle to de-ice the windscreen. Dad would curse while pulling out the choke several times and then when the motor turned over, the car would need to run a few minutes to warm up the engine. Waiting outside the car or in it, our teeth would chatter and we'd be freezing. There was heating in cars but it was not very effective and the vinyl seats that stuck to your legs in summer were terribly cold in winter. Once we were moving, Dad or Mum would carefully nose the car down the hill at Trevallyn. Visibility was almost impossible in fog or heavy rain; cars would suddenly loom up and many near accidents ensued. Roads were sometimes iced over; we did a few 360 degrees spins on the road ice on Bain Terrace in Mum's fiat, which scared us all very much.

Despite the newspaper underneath my artwork, I still managed one time, to spill black Indian ink on the floorboards.

I was nearly two when Marcus was born and some of my earliest recollections are of my mother sitting at her desk drawing pictures of ladies dresses for McKinlays - a big shop in Launceston. Roslyn did music practice, Marcus played cars and I mostly drew nearby. We were also minded by an old couple who treated us as though we were their own grandchildren while Mum worked several days a week at the Examiner.

Mum painted watercolour landscapes and exhibited them with the Launceston Art Society. Sometimes we children went out painting with her which was a very happy thing to do for me. Once we'd done our paintings we could play while she continued to paint.

I loved going with her to the Annual Art Exhibition at the old Queen Victoria Museum.

The AMP and Examiner were the two places where my parents worked. When we were school children we visited Mum or Dad at work sometimes. I would gaze up at the figure with the motto above the entrance as I went in - 'Amicus Sertis Reinsertus', which I later discovered meant, 'a certain friend in troubled times.' Inside there was the solemn, respectful atmosphere of the insurance office. A row of girls in uniforms sat typing in the big office, while men in suits and pork pie hats with shiny briefcases went in and out. They were all representatives selling insurance, just like my Dad, I was told.

The Examiner office was completely different! Mum was Senior Artist at the Examiner. It was a much more interesting place to visit after school or during the school holidays. I loved to sit at the art desk watching the artists working. There was a heap of activity at the Examiner. Mum explained that was because everything was done in a hurry because tomorrow's deadline had to be met. Upstairs in the newsroom, men sat at big machines, noisily turning copy into typeset. The copy boy who was not much older than ourselves, was always rushing to and fro with boxes of 'blocks,' as they were called. They were to be the pictures in the next day's paper! We were lucky to visit Mum at the Examiner.

COLES

We used to love to visit the big Coles shop in the middle of Launceston. Coles had long counters with all sorts of interesting odds and ends. I especially liked the kewpie dolls, tiny plastic fruits and pretty hairclips.

One day when shopping in Coles with Mum, Marcus and I wandered away and sat on the stairs which led to the Cafeteria on the first floor. Looking down we wondered why our Mum was walking up and down the aisles looking worried. She was looking for us!

What a relief it was for her when she looked up toward the stairs and there we were. Mum was so happy to see us.

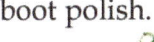ow I envied my brother his winter pyjamas. It was fashionable for girls to sleep in flannelette nighties but I did not like mine at all. We'd say our goodnights, then locate the hot bottle in our icy beds, holding down the nightie's edge with our toes. Hot bottles were often too hot despite Mum making covers for them. Once we'd thawed ourselves out and drifted off to sleep, the trouble began. A few turns and the nightie got twisted and sometimes ended up around your armpits. Brrr, so cold! Half wake up and pull the nightie down, anchor with toes again, fall asleep.

Bed toys were very important to me, just as they are for most children. I had so many for a while that they crowded me almost out of my bed. Often our cat got in too, a fabulous toasty friend!

There were nowhere near as many clothing choices due to the times and the cool winters of Tasmania. When very small, girls were still expected to wear skirts and dresses with sleekies; later it became acceptable for girls to wear slacks, ski pants and eventually jeans like boys. With skirts, there was a 60s fad for witches britches. These were a type of long underwear to mid thigh, that for the fashionable meant seeing the lacy frills under the miniskirts of stylish models. For little girls of Tasmania, they had a far more practical application - to keep frozen bottoms a little warmer!
Wool ruled all forms of warmth in clothing and luckily many people knitted; I had some fabulous jumpers made for me by my Grandma Reynolds. There were no polar fleece or thermals and ski jackets were far different to the modern variety. When quilted parkas and desert boots arrived, they were a really exciting event in clothing, to compliment our scarves, hats and mittens.
I also felt very stylish in my pink jiffies - a kind of cheap elasticised ballet slipper.
With no velcrose, hooks and eyes, press-studs, zips and buttons were used for fastening clothing, along with belts, buckles and braces for boys. Mum, like most people's mothers, sewed our skirts and coats and handmade our summer school uniforms. Shoes were expensive and hand-me-downs were common. We had to learn to tie our shoelaces by the time we went to school and to shine our shoes every week with boot polish.

Like most little girls Roslyn and I were fascinated by Mum's makeup. She bought some bright red nail polish which we really HAD to try out. Unfortunately in our botched attempts at painting our fingernails, the bottle tipped over and spilled. Mum had just finished making us girls lovely pink and grey pussy-willow bedspreads. Rossy's bedspread had nail polish stains on it and we got into trouble!

The line between dreams and reality was very thin sometimes for me. I dreamed things that I was absolutely sure had happened. Always interested in makeup and potions, I dreamed that the white waxy coating on the stamen of Arum lilies was good for beautifying one's skin! When the arum lilies in our garden were in a suitable state, I smeared white pollen all over my face. It was so soft and fine! Half an hour later my face began to swell. For a few days my face was like a puffball from an allergic reaction and I had to concede that my dream was not real!

I also dreamt I lost my grandma's black cut glass beads and felt really guilty for years – only to find they never existed!

Such is the power of dreams.

Children all have nightmares and are left with a fearful feeling from them. Because I had many ear infections and therefore high temperatures, my nightmares were frequent and really awful. Looming colours and shapes that sped up, Daddy laughing at me from the wrong side of the bed and shapeless black monsters that smothered me….

The dark behind the bedroom cupboard could have me paralysed in my bed, imagining some monster there. Not to mention the witch under the bed or the shadowy scratchy scratchy on the blind, which Mum showed me was the tree outside my window, but I never quite believed her.

Other childhood fears and superstitions were related to jetties with holes between the planks, lines on the pavements – either walking between them or on the lines only, peacock feathers, ghosts, black wiggly Saw fly grubs and a very persistent fear of forgetting to put on my underpants and getting to school without them!

Children living on the higher streets of our part of Trevallyn felt a little deprived. On hot summer days we could hear the Mr. Whippy van's melodious 'Greensleeves' playing as the van wheezed up the steep hill. The music would stop and children poured out of their homes to run at breakneck speed down to Bain Terrace; Mr Whippy couldn't make it any further up to our streets and parked just off North Bank in a small lay-by.

We'd extract money from Mum or Dad and run down Kootara Place, hare around the corner into Dandenong Road, meeting many children along the way, all racing with ice cream on our minds and usually Mr. Whippy was very patient.

We'd be in heaven if we got to dawdle back home with our cold sticky ice creams but full of woe if we didn't make it in time. Skinned knees from falling over in the rush were quite common.

If we were utterly stricken, Dad might drive us over to Anderson Street, where access was easier for Mr. Whippy.

Nanna took me with her to the big church at Glen Dhu, when she delivered huge bunches of white Nerine lilies to decorate the church for a wedding. The church was near their home at Talbot Road.

My sister and I attended Sunday School there, dressed our Sunday best with crinkly white hats and net gloves. We were given many colourful texts after we sang songs.

I was so lucky to stay home with Mum instead of going to kindergarten at Trevallyn Primary School. I started school when I was five. My first teacher was Mrs. Logan. We liked to call her 'Loganberry. She was very kind when I was ill with my ear problems. She came to our home numerous times to bring me my schoolwork. Mum could then give me my lessons so I didn't get behind the other children.

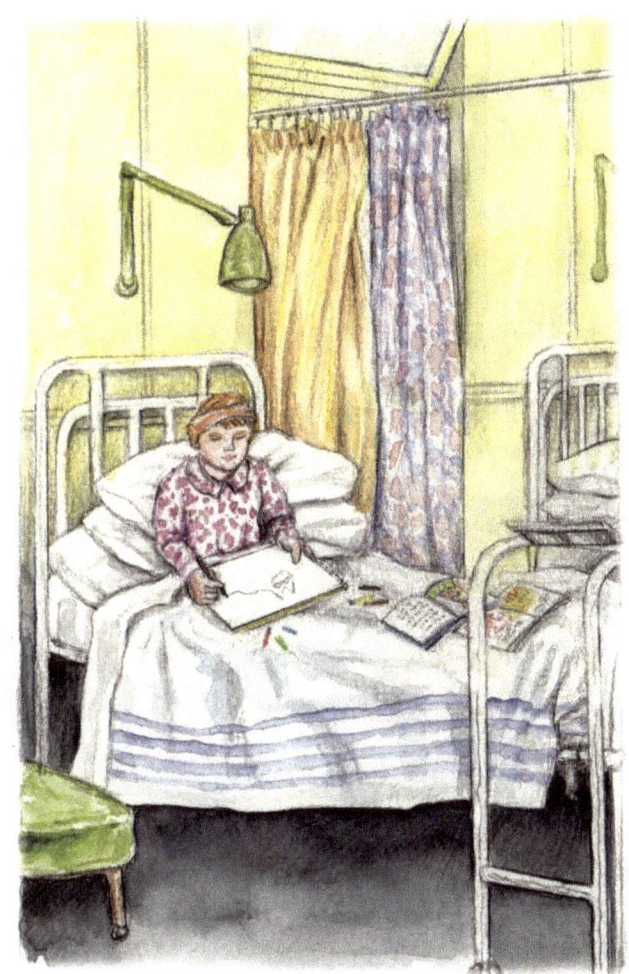

I was terribly unfortunate to have contracted a golden staph infection at birth. My mother also was unlucky. Not much was known about it then so it went unnoticed, although Mum knew something was wrong with me. When finally diagnosed, it was discovered to be in my ears. So off to hospital - many times over.

At seven, a mastoid operation fixed most of my ear troubles; by then I was used to the hospital regime and its loneliness (parents weren't allowed to visit when I was very small). I would read and draw, while nurses and other patients befriended me and praised my art.

It was during the mastoid operation that I was allowed home for a weekend with my head bandaged. Dad, Rossy and Marcus had eaten some Tamar oysters and were all violently ill. Mum hadn't been tempted even though the rocks at low-tide at Hillwood left a harvest for the unwary.

So Mum and I were the well people who looked after them. Then I went back to hospital to finish my recuperation.

Mrs. Logan, our Grade one teacher had the whole grade one class make me get well cards for me. Many of the cards featured the peacocks and peahens. The Cliffgrounds were only a stone's throw away from our school and we were all very impressed with the grand sight of the male birds displaying their gorgeous feathers.

2 x Grade one classes 1965

Here I am in 1965 in Grade one at Trevallyn Primary School, sitting third from the right in the front row. I always sat in the front so I could hear the teacher. We loved school even though discipline was strict and learning by rote was still a mainstay.
As part of a state wide survey to combat enlarged thyroids (not enough iodine in Tassie's soils), many school children were given goitre tablets (potassium iodine) weekly from 1949 to 1965 in Tasmania.
Also from 1951 to 1973 the Free Milk Scheme delivered crates of 1/3 pint bottles of milk to schools daily. We collected the foil milk lids and made decorations from them.
I also recall many dads helped to make an adventure playground in 1969, which included a fabulous flying fox.

Posters with such simple, wholesome catch-phrases adorned the classrooms and corridors - they seemed so colourful when most of our books were black and white with the occasional colour plate in the early 1960s. One great thing about school then, was that homework was not given until about Grade five and most of us learnt what we needed to know without homework.

In the quadrangle behind the school we had our assemblies and special events such as fancy dress parades. Across the road, surrounded by bush was our sports field where all the organised sports were held. We had old-time favourites such as the egg 'n' spoon races and three legged races. Here my friends Keeva Gray and Caroline Watson won the race together while proud mothers and siblings watched.

Sunshine gives us health and energy

Who could forget the fun of elastics, the monkey-bars, the flying fox or swap-cards? Elastics had many levels: ankles, kneesies, thighsies and waists. We'd chant songs and rhymes with special jumping patterns. One was; 'England, Ireland, Scotland, France, inside, outside, inside, out.' At home we could hook our elastic over a chair or two if no one was around to play with.

Swap-cards were also a great craze, with different cards having different values. Some were highly coveted and might need five other cards in return.

When I began school, girl's uniforms were routinely measured to make sure they were only two inches (5cm) above the knee. Strangely they grew shorter and shorter towards the 70s.

In all kinds of weather we walked to and from school except when raining or sleeting heavily. Plastic raincoats were not yet available in the 60s. We would arrive at school with dripping wet hair and damp school uniform from the heavy fogs in winter. Perhaps the teachers taught us through a haze of steam as we slowly dried out.

Needless to say, cleaning out our pockets was a regular chore because they'd be filled with pebbles, pretty leaves, feathers and wilted flowers taken from flowering fences on the way home. I once found the farthing at the top of the back school gate - a birdy treasure.

Sometimes on Saturday morning we had a trip to town with Mum. We went shopping at the delicatessen in the Quadrant. I think it was the first shop of its kind in Launceston. We had never before seen big salamis hanging up or huge wheels of cheese.

Around the corner was the shop we kids loved to visit - Gourlay's lolly shop. it had been there since the 1800s and is still in the heart of Launceston to this day. The whole shop had a lovely sugary fragrance of sweets. My favourites sweets were floral cashews, boiled lollies and lollypops, licorice allsorts, big boss cigars and sherbet fountains. So much to choose from! Mum always bought a little white bag of mixed lollies. What bliss!

At the Launceston Museum an intriguing display to visit was the 'Guan Di temple'. It had been the place of worship for the hundreds of Chinese who worked as miners in the tin mines of North-east Tasmania in the 1880's. We pressed a button on the side of the exhibit and strange music drifted out with a whiff of incense. Colourful Chinese clothes and unusual wall hangings presented a strange experience for me as a girl. It was a window into another culture and another time so different to our own lives.

When we got home from the museum, Mum let me dress up in Grandma Reynolds' blue silk kimono. Marcus decided to dress up as a gangster. The kimono was bought from Shanghai as a present for my great grandmother in 1927, just as the Chinese Civil War broke out.

Under our house Dad rigged up a curtain for a 'stage' over the old building rubble left there - we didn't mind. Big sister Roslyn often organised a heap of kids into dress ups to hold charades and plays there.

There are so many lovely destinations in Tasmania. One day, we packed up the canvas tent and went for a holiday to explore the North West coastal towns and discover the West Coast. Dad checked the tyres and filled up at the Golden Fleece service station in Launceston. We drove west to Deloraine, where we kids got out for a run on the banks of the Meander River. The great Western Tiers had a halo of cloud – would it rain soon I wondered?

At Devonport we tried to see if the RORO, the Roll On - Roll Off Ferry was coming in from Melbourne, which seemed like a distant country to me. We parked and kicked off our shoes to run along the beach and look at the lighthouse painted with curious red and white stripes. Mum took us to see the Aboriginal rock carvings of abalone, periwinkles, emus and seals. The tide was coming in so the blowhole shot water up really high. It was a lovely place to eat our sandwiches looking out into the Bass Strait.

From there we drove up to Stanley, singing songs and eating Dad's liquorice from the glove box. Dad knew it was a fabulous fishing spot; out came the rods so he and Marcus could cast off from the shore. Mum, Rossy and I walked along to the 'nut,' an old volcanic plug perched at the end of the beach. After a happy afternoon (but no fish caught), we drove back to Boat Harbour and ate fish and chips for dinner.

Our final adventure for the day was at Penguin, where Dad and Mum set up the tent next to the beach. It was a long summer evening so we played in the caravan park until it was nearly dark. We all dressed warmly and went to see the fairy penguins as they left the sea to return to their rookeries. Dad had bought his torch with a piece of red cellophane wrapped around it so the little penguins wouldn't be scared and we all had to be very quiet.

After packing up the tent, we drove to Zeehan the next day. The weather had turned cool and it became misty as we travelled south. At the little town of Zeehan we stopped for sandwiches. Mum fed some currawongs our leftovers. Dad took us the new West Coast Heritage Centre. It had all sorts of marvellous gemstones. Dad bought each of us a special wooden ruler and a little glass phial full of peacock ore and fool's gold.

Our Granddad John Reynolds was writing a book called, 'Men and Mines,' when I was little. He told us that the mining industry generated enormous wealth for Tasmania. We wanted to see Queenstown's strange bald hills, caused by mining copper. It seemed baffling to us kids to see such a bare landscape.

We also visited nearby Linda, a ghost town – it felt really strange and spooky with all those empty old buildings and the people all gone.

We stayed the night at the Regatta Point Tavern in Strahan because it had become too wet for camping. Up early and ready to depart at 8 am, we took a trip up a misty Macquarie Harbour. My Dad was very impressed with the J.Lee.M, a 65 ft Huon Pine launch we were travelling on. First we went through Hell's Gates, so named by convicts. Mum told us it was the oldest and most feared penal settlement in Tasmania. The harbour was so beautiful and quiet as we made our way into the Gordon River and up to St John's Fall. Marcus, Roslyn and I darted about the boat taking in the view. I looked for wallabies and birds on the banks, which were covered with dense rainforest. We disembarked and ate lunch at Sarah Island, wandering among the convict ruins. It felt ghostly and we wondered how those prisoners had survived there. We arrived back at Strahan at 4.30 pm. Mum and Dad decided to return to Launceston, a very big drive for us all, but a wonderful adventure.

With a family of five, doing the dishes was a communal affair, although I'm sure Mum did many washing ups herself... To get through it all, we sang songs - old favourites, silly ditties, harmonies, French and 'in the round' songs. Some I recall were, 'Row, row, row your boat,' 'Micheal Finnigan,' 'Edelweiss,' and the 'Skye boat,' song. It made the task seem such fun.

We kids also had many jobs other than washing up. Hanging out and folding washing, shining shoes, shining silver cutlery, cutting the veggies after school to help prepare the evening meal ready, making beds (Roslyn had to make our brother's bed everyday as he was a boy!) and in turn my brother helped wash the car and maintain the boat and lawns with Dad.

My Mum always cooked 'good solid meals' with plenty of fresh fruit and veggies. Even later on when she went to work, we had lovely milk puddings every night. We never bought takeaways but they were not very popular back then. The convenience foods we occasionally had were 'fish fingers' and frozen peas. Mum still regularly used the traditional mincer for soups and shepherd's pie. Then one Christmas, Mum and Dad bought our first modern electrical appliance - the Sunbeam Fry-Pan! Another marvellous help in the kitchen was the arrival of plastic bags. Mum carefully washed them out and dried them on the clothesline for further use.

Possums eating asparagus rolls - remnants from a party.

Getting the lid off the tupperware to eat spaghetti - very funny to see.

On fine nights, particularly in the winter, families of brush tailed possums would let themselves down onto the back verandah from the wattle trees growing nearby. After the washing up had been done, Mum would open the kitchen window and we'd delight in feeding our nocturnal visitors. Always polite, the possums would delicately hold food scraps as they ate. They would lick clean their paws and claws afterwards.

Of course, when we had our dog Sandy, possums mostly stayed away. One night our cat Milko had a standoff on the window sill with a big black possum - Milko arching and hissing, while the possum stood up and tddd -ahed. It was a stalemate and they ignored each other after that.

Watching baby possums grow from pouch bound tiny beings, to young ones holding onto Mama's back was especially thrilling, as was naming them all; 'Twitchet,' 'Old Man,' and 'Ginger' are a couple I remember.

We loved our visitors but Mum and Dad were always thinking up ways to save our veggie garden. The roses were also delicious for them.

Bitey things loomed large in my world, and a healthy respect for these tiny ambassadors of pain was developed early. Aside from bees and wasps in Tasmania there are vicious ants called Jack-jumpers, Inchman and Bull Ants. There are Bluebottle wasps, the Tasmanian Funnelweb Spider, Cave Spiders, Redback spiders and small scorpions. Also in any damp place - leeches and in dry places, ticks. On beaches - Blue Ringed Octopii and of course the three Tasmanian snakes - the Tasmanian Tiger Snake, the Copperhead and the Whipsnake. All this sounds positively scary, but they are mostly just part of the landscape of a Tasmanian child's life to watch out for.

Joyce and I were apt to take our revenge on the local Jack-jumpers. We would find an old tin under her house or mine and make a witch's brews of eggs, dead leaves and insects and anything else we could find. After a few days when it really ponged, we'd pour it over the ant nests nearby.

I did accidentally SIT on an Inchman nest as a little girl. I always took note of where the local ant nests were around the neighbourhood after that!

The highlight of bringing shopping home for me was opening the purple Tuckfield's Ty-nee Tips tea packet to find the lovely bird cards for my albums. Gluing a sought-after card into my albums was such a satisfying pursuit. I had quite a collection and swapped any duplicates - lots of other school friends' families HAD to drink Ty-nee Tips Tea because we kids loved the cards so much. The collection was a valuable source of information about Australian birds and the quality of the artwork was excellent. I still love looking at my bird card albums.

We had a ragged old book with marvellous bird pictures and scratchy old writing in it that I loved to look at. On the wall hung a lovely picture of a bluebird, that I also liked.

I was amazed to learn that the painting and the book were created by some my Mum's relatives from long ago by the name of Lewin.

Grandma Reynolds told me that one of Lewin's sons - J.W. Lewin came to Australia and did many of the first drawings of flowers, animals and Aborigines.

An important event happened in 1966 - we lost the pounds, shillings and pence and in came the dollars and cents. For me, a much more important event that year was when a new family from Scotland moved next door. They had a small girl of my age named Joyce Ivers. We became great friends the minute we met. We both adored animals. We spent many happy hours on the Ivers' tyre swing and rough splintery see-saw where we'd wriggle until we'd be perfectly balanced at each end. We made 'soap' from the hedge out the front of their place. Concocting witch's brews and making mudpies in each other's cubby-houses were also happy pastimes. Joyce's Grandma, always baking in her pinny, would give us homemade Scottish tablet in her flat beneath the main house. It was so yummy.

Joyce was in a class below me at Trevallyn Primary School, but we'd always catch up on the way home so we could watch Kimba the White Lion, Tarzan or Mr. Ed on TV before our playtime.

In Summer, Joyce, Marcus and I had endless fun whirling round and screaming in their paddling pool.

We had an idyllic childhood living as we did with our garden running down to the track to the Cliff Grounds in Trevallyn. Apart from the obvious dangers of falling from rocks, scratches or stubbed toes, us kids just roamed around having adventures. I don't think our parents even considered we could come to harm - after all, when they were children, they had been allowed to wander in the bush just like us. There was a marvellous system of supervision where older kids looked after younger ones until they in turn became old enough to be carers themselves. Pets often came too and our dog Sandy became very good at rock-climbing.

While our parents were busy, us kids were doing important stuff like catching tadpoles, finding clay pans, building dams, testing out newly made billy carts on the bush track and creating collective myths and stories about the bush around us.

The bush was a fabulous place for our imaginations. While out exploring our pets often came too. Sandy, our Cocker Spaniel found a cave, so of course it was named 'Sandy's cave.'

Our white cat Milko often travelled with us. Near Sandy's cave was a heap of rocks we named 'Milko's maze.'

My best friend's dachshund Quilt also came along, skittering through the undergrowth with Sandy. A tall pile of rocks proudly became 'Quilt's castle.'

'Death Valley' in the Cataract Gorge bushland reserve, was a steep, dark valley that received little sun. It was very slippery, ending in rocks that dropped steeply onto the Gorge's walking track. It was easy to lose your footing and go for a tumble, so on this day we left our little brother Marcus safely on the rocks above. As several kids in the gang began exploring, my little brother began to shout. Roslyn, the oldest, called back to him, saying we'd only be a little while longer.

Marcus became very upset and with the strength beyond his years, picked up a huge rock and hurled it down at us, hitting our dog Sandy on his ribs. We knew of course he did not mean to hurt anyone. At his age he would not have realised the effect of his actions.

With the bush at the end of our backyards, it was inevitable that we'd find injured wildlife. Often we'd bring home birds or blue-tongued lizards, or a bandicoot and try to nurse them back to health. As we knew very little about hurt or shocked native fauna, many creatures died in the shoeboxes our mums provided. Dressed in black lace, we would hold a wake and bury them with a twig cross.

We were avid animal lovers. In 1961 there was a drive to interest school-children in a new organisation - World Wide Fund for nature. Of course we both joined and loved the news cards we received about animal rescues.

A success story was a baby possum we named 'Leina,' found by Joyce's dachshund. After a few months Leina was successfully returned to the wild. Mrs. Ivers was relieved as the juvenile possum had taken to climbing up and shredding their living room curtains.

For pets and wildlife, living next to the bush reserve had a sad side. Our caged Zebra and Chestnut Breasted Finches were sometimes meals for kookaburras and currawongs who mesmerized them and pulled the birds through the bars.

While taking Grandma Reynolds for a walk down the bush track, Mum paused by a tree. Looped over the branch above her head was a green snake! We realised later it was a White Lipped or Whip snake and being bitten was unlikely, just scary.

In our garage, a small Ringtail Possum found a hidey hole for winter - in the old wheelbarrow under a tarpaulin. Mum shooed it out several times but it somehow snuck in again until Mum gave up and let it stay. We also had swallows nesting in the garage every year, which was lovely.

We occasionally found old traps in the bush and marked where they were to tell Dad, who would take them away. Sadly we learnt of the cruelty of illegally set traps when our lost cat came home missing most of her front paws. It was a very sad day for all of us.

Roller-skating was a big passion for kids in the neighbourhood and being kids we had to find the steepest street to skate down. Trevallyn is very hilly, so we would walk or skate down Kootara Place, meeting kids along the way. We would converge at the top of a little lane called Wattle Way.

Wattle Way is so steep that it has rails to one side for people to grasp as they toil to the top of the lane. For learner skaters, the rails gave some security on their way down as they could grab on and stop at any time because roller skates did not have any brakes on them.

More seasoned skaters grabbed the rail at the very end after skating down the hill at maximum speed. Added to the exhilaration of speed, was a sense of fear, because Wattle Way led onto a busy Bain Terrace.

Kootara Place, where we lived was a quiet cul-de-sac high up in Trevallyn. It was a perfect street for children's after school games with very little traffic. The boys played cricket and drove their home-made billy carts. We had skipping ropes, elastics and yo-yo's. There was always a selection of bikes, trikes and scooters to ride.

Even on cold winter afternoons there were kids to be found out and about our neighbourhood. When we saw the daddies arriving home driving up the street, we knew it meant that soon there would be the call to come in to wash our hands to have dinner. Homework was done after dinner and often in Summer we went out again to make mud pies or play spooks in the twilight.

Like most children, I had my fair share of scrapes, bumps and bruises from playing outside. We were all smeared with Mecurochrome, a dubious topical antiseptic which dyed your skin bright red for days. Even when indoors because of the weather, we would be busy with many activities. My sister loved dolls, especially an English walking doll called Isobelle, bought back from London and inherited from our Aunt Judy. Barbie dolls were becoming very popular though many disapproved of her figure. Roslyn had some Skipper dolls, supposedly Barbie's sister. I could never take dolls seriously because when quite young we managed to fry the hair off some in front of the indoor heating and they looked awful. We loved to make pompoms, play Barrel 'o' Monkees, Checkers, pick-up-Sticks and Monopoly. With our Mum and Dad being creative, we children could help ourselves to lots of art materials as well.

On rainy days Joyce and I played on the Ivers' verandah. There we created our own fantasy worlds. Out of dirt, branches and water we built make-believe farms, paddocks and mountains. We then filled the landscape with our collection of smal plastic animals. We created dens at the end of the verandah out of timber crating, cardboard, old sheets and bedspreads and pretended to be our favourite animals and got really good at hurrying around on all fours!

How utterly exciting it was to get my first packet of felt-pens. Felt-pens were so astounding and rapidly overtook coloured pencils for our early artistic efforts.

Roslyn, my big sister had learned music since she was six years old. Often we sat on her bed as she played the guitar. I remember Joyce and I singing along with her songs such as 'House of the Rising Sun', the 'Ball Bearing Bird', 'I get by with a little help from my Friends', 'Times they are a-changing', 'Motherless Child' and 'Will the Circle Be Unbroken'. We would all sing along, swept away by the passion of the songs as she played her guitar.

From most places in Launceston, residents are aware of the Ben Lomond National Park as every day the sun rises over its impressive bulk. A lovely winter day trip with my friend Joyce, took us up to the top of Ben Lomond in Joyce's dad's old Holden panel van. When I arrived from next door in my mum's mittens, a pompom hat and scarf, Mr Ivers was putting chains on the car wheels to make sure we didn't slip on the icy roads.

The Ivers who were from Scotland, took a great interest in their new Tasmanian surroundings.

'Ben Lomond was named after a Scottish mountain by the same name,' Mrs Ivers told Joyce and I, while her husband drove with great care up Jacob's Ladder, the sharp hairpin bends throwing us giggling girls about in the van.

When we got to the top, Joyce and I built a big snowman and had a snowball fight. Mr and Mrs Ivers took photos and shared a thermos of cocoa and some sandwiches, before we headed back to Launceston.

As a young couple with a new house in a new area, my mum and dad held many barbeques. Dad constructed a barbeque out of left over bessa blocks from building the house and a sheet of iron he found. Mum made a fringed orange raffia cover for the hills hoist for those moments where there might be a sprinkle of rain during the festivities.

Being so far south, the Tasmanian summer makes up for the long winter and it stays light until 9.15pm. Parents and children often stayed out for late picnic dinners or barbeques. While the parents partied, Roslyn would gather up all the children and we'd have madcap games of chasies through the garden, hide 'n' seek outside and inside and play spooks in the growing dark. We'd raid the finger foods, eat a snag on white bread and generally disrupt the parents with our noise and chaos.

Other unexpected visitors to our new house were peacocks, which wandered up from the Cliffgrounds in search of food. We ould hear their haunting call coming through the bush and we'd run down to our backyard with some bread for them.

Occasionally in the summer, Dad decided it would be nice to take a picnic down to the Cliffgrounds. Mum would tell us three to change into good clothes whilst she made sandwiches and filled up a thermos to put into a cane wash-basket. Sometimes we took homemade ginger beer - yum! It was rare to take Sandy, who would get too excited so he was generally left at home. We'd pile into the car and in five minutes be at the carpark.

Down the long flights of steps to the Cliffgrounds Tea Rooms we'd walk. They were set in beautiful green lawns with gardens of azaleas and rhododendrons. On the banks higher up were walks through maple trees and huge Californian pine trees. Strutting through the gardens were peacocks, peahens and guinea fowl. I was in seventh heaven when I found peacock feathers.

After our picnic lunch the family went to the little shop at the tea-rooms and bought ice-creams. We were then allowed to take off our good clothes as our swimsuits were underneath and we would race across the suspension bridge to splash around in the First Basin swimming pool. It was often very crowded but the water was not deep; no-one ever considered it dangerous. I loved our Summer days at the Cliffgrounds and Cataract Gorge.

In Launceston we all knew what a lot of fun it was crossing from the Cliffgrounds side of the South Esk to the First Basin on the suspension bridge. Kids of all ages ran from side to side causing the whole bridge to sway. When the river was in flood it was even more scary-fun, but we still had to do it!

In Summer there was rarely too much water to stop us crossing the stepping stones lower down below the very deep First Basin - a very large contained semi-lake we were told was 'bottomless' and people had dived in never to be seen again! One of my Dad's Wheatley cousins as a young man tried out his snorkel in the Second Basin, an equally deep body of water and disappeared! So naturally we children never tested the story. The rocks were quite slippery and it was easy to lose your balance so many kids helped each other across and we were very careful.

My mum and her friends, all good swimmers, did swim across the First Basin once, but never again as they said it was terribly cold. I think my sister did laps there, brave girl.

In Spring Joyce and I would eagerly gallop down the hill from Trevallyn, noticing the new crocus flowers, buds, baby wallabies and peacock chicks.

In Winter, though very cold, it didn't stop us visiting. The trees looked very bare, but we didn't mind at all. It was and still is, a marvellous place for adventures. In Spring, Joyce and I would eagerly gallop down the hill from Trevallyn, noticing the new crocus flowers, buds, baby wallabies and peacock chicks. Summer was all about the Basin and the river, keeping cool in the heat. In Autumn, Joyce and I knew where to find deciduous European trees - maples, ash and oaks with their colourful leaves. We took a wheelbarrow down the rough bush track to the Cataract Gorge Cliffgrounds one autumn. We filled up our barrow with leaves then heaved, pushed and pulled it back up the hill to our backyard at Trevallyn. Once there we built a lovely big pile of leaves and jumped up and down on it. What a reward for all our work.

Such simple fun!

The Cliffgrounds and Cataract Gorge were like a second home for me. Joyce and I visited a few times a week, running down the bush track from home to emerge on the roadway. From there we could go anywhere for our adventures. We might just pick up feathers in the secret place where the peacocks roosted. We might cross the South Esk by jumping across the bridge or pick our way across the stepping stones. We often encountered blue tongue lizards, echidnas, wallabies and bandicoots, all the while listening to the bright birdsong of wrens, kookaburras, shrikes, thrush and parrots.

Sometimes it was just to wander the paths to the various sun splattered bowers surrounding the tea rooms, where we could look for orchids or mushrooms or watch the river. Perhaps we'd trail our fingers over the shimmery azaleas and rhododendrons or pretend to be musicians in the Victorian band rotunda.

The moods of the South Esk River varied from benign and gentle to powerfully violent. In summer the river was delightfully passive. Joyce and I would take am old leather backpack with sandwiches and hike up the river to Duck Reach. There was a path running along the side of the river from the First Basin to the equally deep Second Basin further up. By climbing down from the track, Joyce and I found our way rock hopping all the way, sometimes swimming or paddling in the shallows. So frequent were our journeys that we had a special waterhole we claimed as OURS! We had such freedom.

We were still living in Summerhill when there was an unusually high flood. Dad took us along the road overlooking the Second Basin. With other amazed spectators we watched the flood crest arrive and completely engulf the suspension bridge across the river, washing it away! It only took the blink of an eye. Dad said the bridge was part of the very first power station which was built at Duck Reach a long time ago.

Sometimes in winter we'd be woken in the night by the river as it breached Trevallyn Dam and thundered down the gorge.

A huge fire burnt the bush near our house at Trevallyn, though I think that West Launceston had received the worst of it. The carefully maintained fire break behind the houses helped Trevallyn's homes to survive. Nevertheless most of the area around the Basin was badly burnt out. The fire may have been one of the many fires that affected the whole of Tasmania in the summer of 1967.

Despite the choking smoke and heat, it was terribly exciting! The Launceston firemen in their big black helmets and double breasted woollen tunics hosed down the trees in our backyard and put out spot fires that jumped the break all along the back of our homes. Neighbours from streets over joined the fight with wet hessian bags tied to broom and rake handles.

Garden hoses were in full use against sparks catching alight in the undergrowth. Marcus and I rushed back and forth from the firemen to the front gate, to look at the Launceston Fire Brigade parked over our driveway. They connected up to the mains water supply and dragged their enormous fire hoses down to the backyard.

A fireman offered to let Marcus hold the hose - Marcus was thrilled, until the recoil from the water pressure knocked him right over.

After Christmas, Cracker night and the Show were the most exciting events for children. Cracker night was held on the Queen's birthday long weekend. There'd usually be a large bonfire in the local park with neighbours gathering to enjoy it. Generally parents lit the fireworks for our safety, but we children were given pennybangers to throw down and frighten each other with. The most magical crackers I recall were the lovely Catherine Wheels, Roman Candles and Sky Rockets. We'd scream and run about and when the excitement got too much, we could curl up in Mum's lap and enjoy the bonfire.

The Launceston Show was a huge affair with lots of rides, fairyfloss and free showbags. There were fabulous displays of rural produce, handcrafts and livestock. I loved the wood chopping competitions where the quickest man won and I adored the baby animal displays. There were crowds of folks queued up to win a prize throwing ping-pong balls into clown's mouths or have another go at the shooting gallery. The carousel, cups 'n' saucers and Ferris wheel were terribly exciting for little kids, whilst dodgem cars and a ghost train provided thrills for the older ones.
I won my first art prize at the show for a painting of two horses.

In 1963 Queen Elizabeth II visited all the states including Tasmania. We stood with the crowd on the Cataract Bridge to watch her wave as she passed by in her car. It was a fairy tale moment for many children, especially little girls, who consequently dreamed about being princesses for a long time afterwards.

We were big fans on the Drive-In. We often went to the Mowbray Drive-In in Launceston and the Elwick Drive-In in Hobart. We would hurry through dinner and our bath and into our pyjamas, dressing gowns and slippers. Taking our pillows and favourite teddies, we kids would pile into the car while Dad and Mum stowed blankets and drinks. At the Drive-In, Dad would locate a park and get as close to the speaker pole as he could. Dad would unhook the speaker and feed it through the driver's window, to hook on top of the glass. Mum would take us to queue with many other excited kids in dressing gowns and slippers at the shop for popcorn before the film.

Once snugged up in the car, the film would begin and we'd settle in to enjoy the movie. If the sound was crackly or there were boring bits, kissy bits or we just got tired, we could doze or fall asleep in a cosy nest of blankets on the back seat. On cold nights the windows often became fogged up, so Dad swiped the windscreen with the wipers every so often until the end of the film.

Another marvellous place to go to was the Princess Theatre in Launceston. Mum took us to see the ballets, Swan Lake and The Nutcracker there when we were very small. I fell asleep during both of them and I am afraid to say, that has coloured my perception of ballet ever since.

We went to see many popular movies there. It was where I fell in love with Julie Andrews in The Sound of Music and Elsa the lioness in Born Free. I loved 101 Dalmations, Jungle Book, Mary Poppins and Doctor Dolittle, to name a few. Before the feature there was usually an interesting newsreel and some Loony Tunes cartoons.

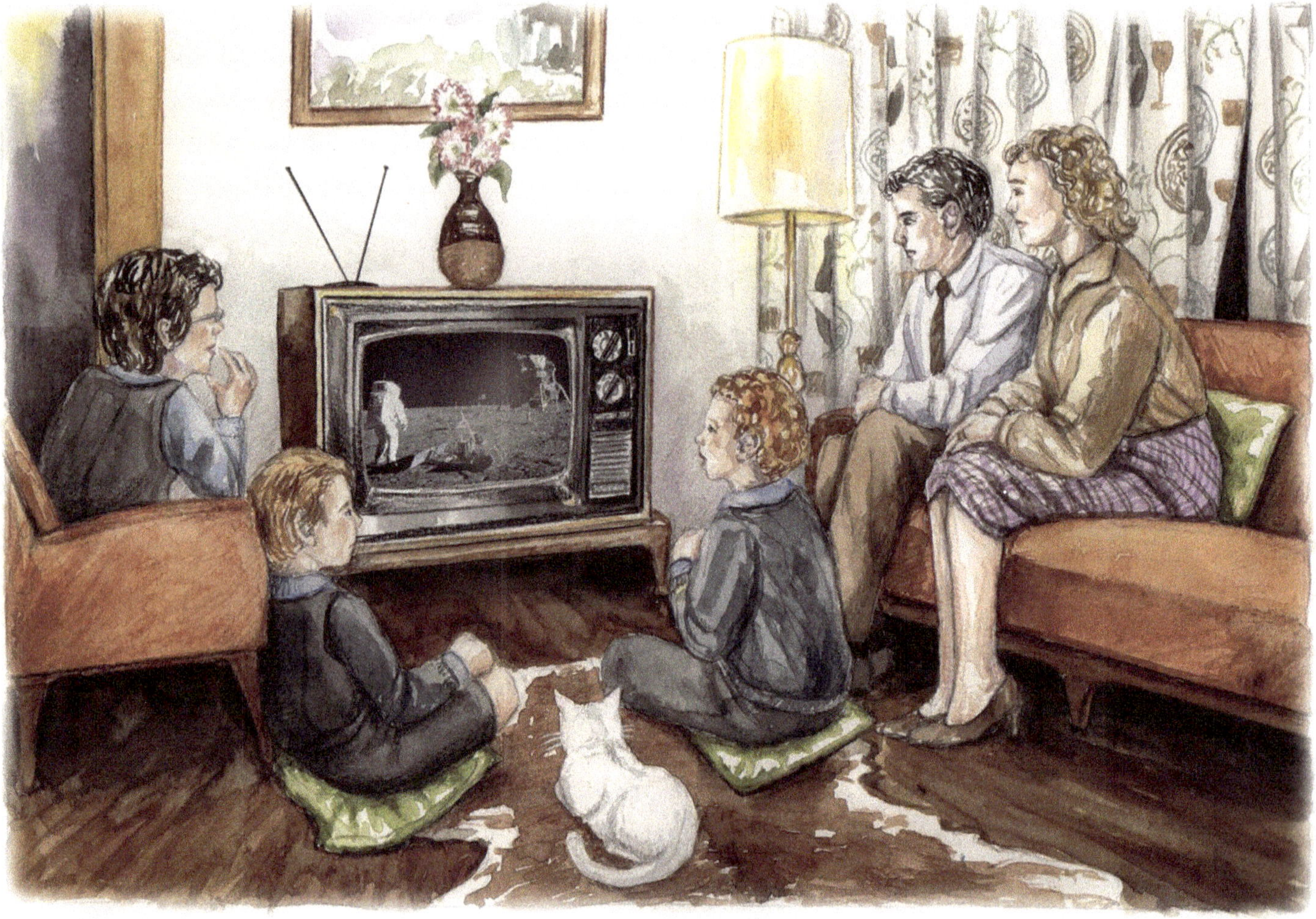

We watched Neil Armstrong, the first human to walk on the moon in 1969, on our black and white television, was also an astonishing event. Some of my school chums stayed at school to watch the event and some came home to watch it. Along with an estimated 600 million people - the largest global audience at that time we all watched with amazement.

Of course wearing colanders on our heads and making costumes from Mum's aluminium tin foil became extremely popular. Some children even acquired goldfish bowls big enough to put their heads in and were much admired as astronauts although they did sound funny.

The EXAMINER

ASTRONAUTS TAKE FIRST MOON STEPS

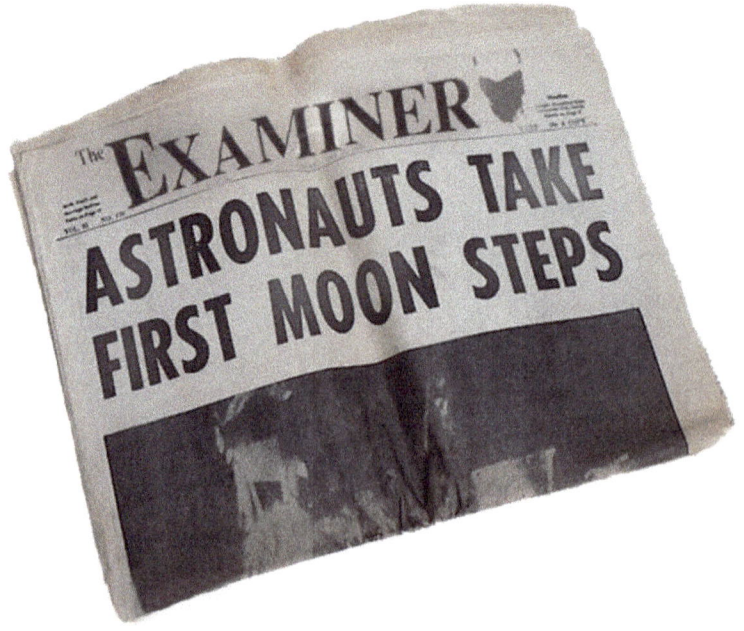

As part of the first generation of Australian kids to have black and white television to entertain us, we were exposed to a diet of mainly American shows each afternoon as this box began to dominate the lounge room. Joyce and I would rush home from school to watch Adventure Island and Kimba before homework and playing outside. We never missed a Tarzan movie and Joyce would yodel like Tarzan to call me out to play from my house. We also went to the movies (Born Free and Sound of Music were my favourites). We had few children's EP records we were allowed to put on the turntable and listened to children's shows on the radio.

Who could forget Annette Funicello in the Mickey Mouse Club? Whilst Queen Elizabeth II visiting Launceston was a sweet fairytale, Annette Funicello seemed something like royalty to us too and she came to our lounge rooms everyday! Children were all thrilled with the Mickey Mouse Club on our black and white televisions and devoured episodes for dissection in the playground the next day. Annette stole everyone's hearts with her sweet face and lovely singing. Girls wanted to look and be like her and she was for some boys, their first 'puppy love.'

Just a bit younger than Roslyn or I, Marcus took to television and loved watching as much as he could. We were all very susceptible to the advertising on TV, but Marcus was very influenced by the first fads for children. His first words were, 'mi….ey mow.' He had to wear his Mickey Mouse ears everywhere. If when we went shopping, we passed Mickey Mouse merchandise, he would get very upset if Mum passed by without buying something. When very small, he would fall down on the shop floor in a tantrum, once holding his breath until he went purple, Mum said.

A doctor friend assured Mum that he'd seen many children having fits about Mickey Mouse, who never knew what a huge influence he was!

Spoilt for swimming choice in Launceston, we could go either to the Basin or Windmill Hill Swimming Pool. After getting changed, we had to run through a freezing cold ankle bath of disinfectant that lay between the change room and the pool. Feet seemed to be suspect, yet not the rest of our bodies.

At the pool we could happily play and have a picnic under the umbrella and of course, ice cream! Lessons and learning proper stroke technique, laps swimming and squad racing were also available. These were more the province of my sister Roslyn, who was a top swimmer and did training at the pool. She would happily do thirty laps at a time and loved doing lifesaving medals like the bronze medallion and silver star, as well as simulated rescues.

Ear problems delayed my learning to swim. Mum was a strong swimmer and would take Marcus and I out past the wavelets at Bridport. She would breaststroke with us both hanging from her neck. She taught me the basics and at high school there were weekly swimming lessons in the warmer months. Often I'd succumb to dizzy spells and start drowning a little as my sense of balance went topsy-turvy. I was not spared however, and competed in many swimming carnivals.

By December each year, everyone's thoughts were about Christmas shopping. Town was full of mums meeting the kids after school, planning presents for the family and all the extended families. It was a very serious business with a great deal of pretence about what Father Christmas might bring. Sometimes we had 'tried it on already'!
On the corner of Brisbane and St. John Street was a giant Santa with a welcoming finger.

I remember with fondness those Christmasses when we sang carols in our lounge room while Roslyn accompanied us on the piano. Mum played violin while Marcus and I sang or played our recorders.

A weekend before Christmas Day we journeyed to the North-East to the pine forest on the top of the Sideling near Scottsdale. We went to get a (highly illegal) pine tree! However, Dad never cut down a tree, he just sawed of a few branches to tie together to form a suitable Christmas tree shape. Dad had worked as a window-dresser when younger and really knew how to make a glamorous Christmas tree. We would decorate it with Mum's lovely Czechoslovakian glass baubles... very carefully.

Dad also pinned pretty foil stars all over the timber wall in our lounge room. How we loved Christmas!

I loved finding shiny Christmas beetles too.

When we were kids we often travelled up and down the Midlands Highway between Launceston and Hobart. We couldn't wait to see the disappearing house at Conara, which seemed to sink and vanish behind a small hill.

At Ross, when the river was up, cars would carefully travel one way on a wooden jetty-like viaduct to pass over the flooded area - it would take ages!

By Oatlands the next big highlight was watching out for little animals carved out of small hedges and to guess what they were.

It seemed such a long way. I would often close my eyes on the journey and let the sunlight flickering through trees passing by create a kaleidoscope of colours on the inside of my eyelids.

One time on our regular trip on Boxing Day, it snowed while we were driving - in the middle of summer! On another chillier occasion driving at night, Mum roused us from our sleep to show us the sky - all lit up with the Southern Aurora Borealis - unforgettable!

When I was quite small I remember always looking up at Mount Wellington as soon as it came in sight when we were driving down from Launceston. In the summer the mountain looked all pale with the sun on it. The pretty heath and pink mountain berries would be out and on a visit to the top we could see for miles and miles!

In the winter clouds came down and covered the mountain. When the clouds lifted there was the snow! Dad would put chains on the tyres and we'd drive up the mountain as far as we could - so did many other families with kids. The road had been built by poor unemployed men in the 1930s who sometimes didn't even have good shoes in the cold, Mum told us. We would be glad of our good shoes and woolly jumpers, scarves and gloves.

When we got out of the car, what did it matter if it was cold; we had a lovely time playing in the snow, shivering and shouting with excitement. We would take bottles and billies to collect cold mountain water from one of the many waterfalls.

On the way up Huon Road to Ferntree was another place where in a sandstone quarry we sometimes dug out marvellous fossils of sea shells and corals that looked like ferns. I was amazed to think it was all under water once.

Merrington, Knocklofty terrace, West Hobart

Driving to Hobart for the weekend, we'd often arrive drowsy on the Friday evening, to be put to bed at my grandparents' big house 'Merrington.' My brother and I would be top-n-tailed on an old couch in the sun-room. When older we transferred to old bedrooms to sleep on the beds Mum and her brothers had as children. My sister, who had lived with our grandparents when she was a baby, had my Aunt Judy's old room nearby, complete with shutters and a chamber pot. We'd wake to sidle out past the kitchen to the outside toilet, which faced a courtyard and high sandstone retaining wall. If you needed to go out at night it would be very creepy with the big trees on the wall blowing in the wind. Roslyn told Marcus and I spooky stories about the witch's house next door and a haunted house with a burnt out window nearby, so we were quite frightened. Next we'd often pile into my Grandma Yaya's single bed and secretly eat her Chlorophyll tablets while Daddad, my Grandpa read passages out of the newspaper to her from his single bed. In the big kitchen the radio played while Mum, Grandma and sometimes our aunties made breakfast. It was often followed by a tour around the garden, patting the cats Bobby and Buttons and feeding little bits of fruit and lettuce to the Eastern Rosella in the cage on the front porch. We loved the Monkey Puzzle tree planted by Great Grandma Reynolds and all the rhododendrons and fruit trees which were marvellous for playing hide-n-seek. We could dash along the top of the high sandstone wall past the cherry and bay trees, the Guelder pompom tree and peer up at the witch's house, seemingly benign during the day. Built by the Waterworths at the same time as Merrington, it was one of the grandest homes in Hobart in its day - it even had a full sized pipe-organ.

kitchen bathroom toilet old laundry

We'd play chasey through the hall with its draped curtains and lovely glass wind chime, around the funny old hall stand with umbrellas and coats and past the ancient black telephone that hardly ever rang. Perhaps we could hide behind the door in the old pink bathroom which smelt of Daddad's shaving cream, or under the table in the dining room. While the adults were busy in the formal lounge room, we'd climb the kitchen bench to eat cashews and dried apricots, which were such luxuries then. I would admire Yaya's fabulous flower displays in old fashioned vases or wander along the bookshelves full of old books with gilt lettered spines. These are some of the things I remember most from our happy times in Hobart.

My grandparent's home in Knocklofty Terrace was up an incredibly steep hill and the shop selling bread and milk was down at the bottom. A daily chore was to race down the hill for Grandma and sometimes we'd try walking backwards to make the going easier on our way home. There were huge bushes of fennel halfway up and I loved chewing it.

The view was wonderful and we could always see so much activity on the Derwent. If it was a fine day a flotilla of boats would be out racing in the wind. In the afternoons the sea breeze would roll up the Derwent and it would become all hazy. Sometimes we might see the Bridgewater Jerry, a big fog that rolled out over the Derwent.

Sometimes we'd walk along to Constitution Dock from the city centre of Hobart. Children could run along the wharves while the adults took a leisurely promenade behind us admiring the boats. One Christmas Marcus was very excited to receive a new fishing rod and proudly cast in there for the first time.

Often we'd walk over to Salamanca Place (there were no markets started there until 1971) and we knew that our Granddad had his office there. We would walk up Kelly Steps to the swings at Arthur's Circus in Battery Point. There is a small circular village green with swings in the middle where we could play.

Another lovely trip we liked was to drive the scenic route through Sandy Bay and Taroona to the Shot Tower. Dad told us that shot was made for guns by dropping molten lead from the top into a bucket of water at the bottom. We climbed the spiral stairs inside to look at the fabulous view from the top.

We made a special trip to Hobart one year to meet our cousins from Queensland. They had been living in London but had moved to Townsville. John and Anna were younger than Marcus and I, but having travelled so much seemed very grown up. For us it was a novelty to meet people from way 'over there.' We all ran down the big hill and into town where we showed them the new Cat and Fiddle arcade. On the hour the, 'Hey, diddle diddle, the cat and the fiddle...' tune rang out to the joy of awaiting children. The cat played a big fiddle, the cow jumped the moon and the dish and spoon ran away. We were all so excited seeing this marvel.

Uncle David had a workshop under the house where he created real flying model aeroplanes. They were painted in bright colours with big numbers on the wings. Uncle David's overalls were always covered in bits of balsa wood and tissue paper scraps stuck on with Tarzan's grip. He loved showing Marcus his creations but didn't really encourage visitors to his workshop.

I loved seeing all the partly built planes, the tools, machinery, propellers and fuel tanks when I was invited.

Yummy! How could I ever forget going on a tour of the Cadbury factory at Claremont? We joined a group of children and parents to be shown through the astonishing process of making Cadbury chocolates. We watched the vast vats of chocolate being poured into hundreds of moulds for fillings and additions. The chocolates went through many machines to be sorted and packaged. All the children received a bag of chocolate at the end to enjoy- wow!

Our grandfather John Reynolds collected stamps. We would talk to him about them as he sat at a card-table with his magnifying glass and stamp tweezers, peering at beautiful stamps from all over the world and carefully putting them in albums. He had a lovely collection of semi-precious rocks like rose quartz and peacock ore, which seemed so amazing to me. Minerals from the West Coast and wonderful fossils added to this collection.

Making jam and preserves every fruit season was a traditional pastime at Merrington. Once the house had been attached to a large orchard but my time there were apricot, nectarine, plum, peach, green gage, fig, red current, cherry, walnut, as well as raspberry and loganberry canes and a gooseberry bush. I enjoyed climbing the trees with a basket to pick fruit. Back down in the big kitchen it would be a hive of industry for a few days. Someone would be sent to get the preserving jars and clips so bottled fruit could be made for winter.

Summer at my Grandma's seemed awash with sugar and fruit as the scent of boiling jam lingered all over the house.

One time I thought I'd be a helpful girl and tidy up Yaya's spice shelf. I didn't realise she had the jars placed in a way she could find them by feel and memory due to her near blindness. We heard later she had made a cake with curry powder... I felt so awful about it for ages after.

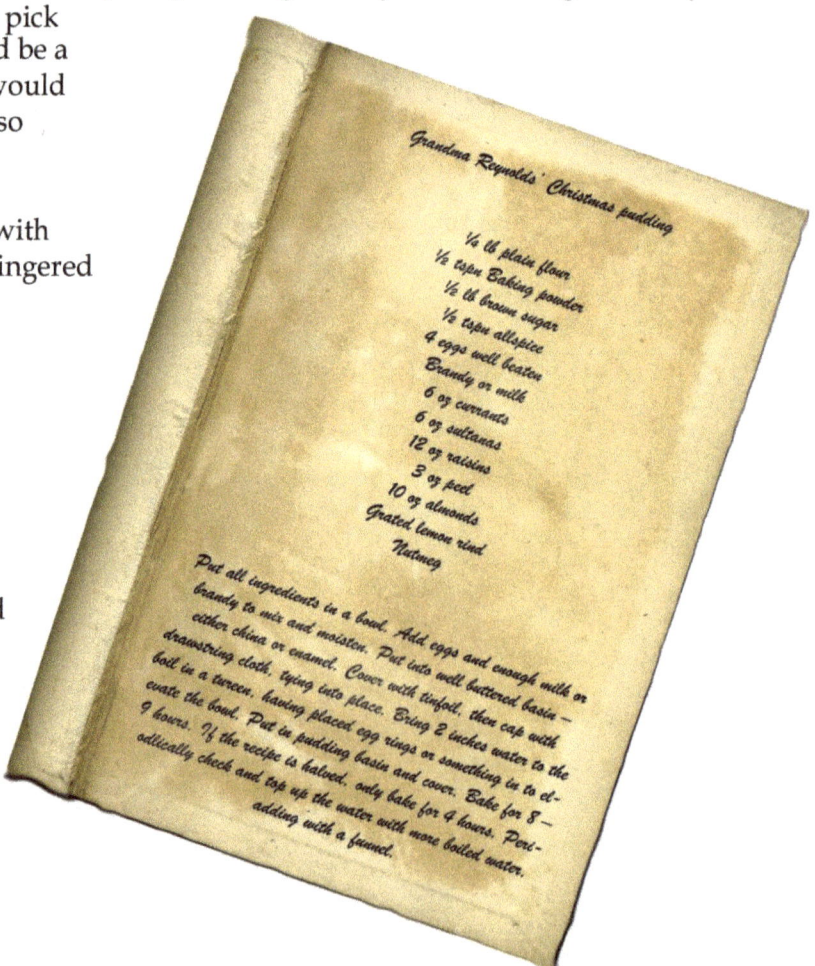

Grandma Reynolds' Christmas pudding

½ lb plain flour
½ tspn Baking powder
½ lb brown sugar
½ tspn allspice
4 eggs well beaten
Brandy or milk
6 oz currants
6 oz sultanas
12 oz raisins
3 oz peel
10 oz almonds
Grated lemon rind
Nutmeg

Put all ingredients in a bowl. Add eggs and enough milk or brandy to mix and moisten. Put into well buttered basin – either china or enamel. Cover with tinfoil, then cap with drawstring cloth, tying into place. Bring 2 inches water to the boil in a tureen, having placed egg rings or something to elevate the bowl. Put in pudding basin and cover. Bake for 8 – 9 hours. If the recipe is halved, only bake for 4 hours. Periodically check and top up the water with more boiled water, adding with a funnel.

Dinnertime every Saturday when we visited was always a roast dinner. Our grandma was used to catering for a large number and was a wonderful cook. On special occasions when there were many family members, we children sat at a card-table beside the big one.

I remember we had most Christmas dinners there in Hobart. Our mum and grandma bought to the table a magnificent spread with all the trimmings. We had crackers to pull with little paper party hats and other little toys inside. When Christmas pudding arrived - a huge family size, we had slice after slice to try to get more threepences or sixpences hidden in the pudding.

Serviettes and table manners were expected and social decorum was aided by homilies and sayings from a different age. so despite a little bickering we children behaved as beautifully as we could. Afterwards when we were very full, we kids helped to 'put away' the washing up and Granddad helped with the drying up - all made fun with lots of singing in the kitchen.

> Please remember if you are able...
> To keep your elbows off the table.

An exciting annual event was the Sydney to Hobart Yacht Race which started in Sydney on Boxing Day every year and finished at Constitution Dock in Hobart. For the contestants it was and still is a difficult race with the challenges of unpredictable wind and seas.

We were so lucky to be able to see the beginning and progression of the race on our black and white televisions for the first time in the 1960s.

Some years the weather was kind but others, oh! A Southerly Buster might blow up or unruly conditions on nearby Bass Strait might affect the sailing on the Tasman Sea. Many yachts would retire at Bega, NSW before the going became too rough, so when the first yacht came up the Derwent River we were all in awe of the skill that enabled the crews to make it to Hobart in the big yachts. All of Hobart would take to vantage points around the harbour or those fortunate enough to have boats could motor or sail out to chaperone the yachts in.

Down at Constitution Dock crew then celebrated with friends and family while spectators like us wandered about looking with admiration at the marvellous big yachts.

Our family was lucky enough to have a speedboat up north but we had to satisfy our yachty inspiration with making boats out of corks, newspaper, egg cartons or balsa wood. We sailed them in Grandma's old silver bucket on the verandah.

Port Arthur was a place we all looked forward to visiting. Grandma and Mum made lots of sandwiches for lunch and we all crammed into the car, Marcus and I on our grandparents' knees and Roslyn in between. It was windy when we drove across Eaglehawk Neck. Dad said caravans had been blown off the road there. We stopped to look at the Blowhole where the water sprayed up very high and Roslyn, Marcus and I screamed with delight. We had morning tea at the Devil's Kitchen and were amazed by the Tesselated Pavement. After a quick lunch on arrival at Port Arthur, we joined a tour of the old buildings left from the penal colony. The church with no roof was amazing but I felt all the ghostly sadness in that place. It was a sobering history lesson for any child.

There are many islands dotted around Tasmania, the main ones being Flinder's and King Islands in the Bass Strait and Maria and Bruny Islands in the south. While staying in Hobart one holiday, we drove south and took the car ferry across to Bruny Island from Kettering. Bruny Island had and still has lovely unspoilt places that Tasmanians and visitors are lucky to enjoy. All the beaches were beautiful and Mum actually found a perfect Paper Nautilus shell.

We had a picnic at Adventure Bay and went for a bushwalk, finding some lovely wildflowers. As I was a bird-mad little girl, I was in heaven seeing so many seabirds, yellow wattle-birds, small finches, wrens and parrots. I was sure I saw a Forty Spotted Pardelote and told Mum about it again and again! We chased each other through a natural rock arch on the beach and were terribly excited to see snowy white Bennett's Wallabies, that were tame enough to feed.

Driving north up the East Coast, we took a ferry across the Mercury Strait to Maria Island for the day to look at the Painted Cliffs, sandstone stained with iron oxide, Dad told us. We gathered some fossil fragments at the Fossil Cliffs and looked at the remains of the first penal settlement around Darlington, the main uninhabited town there. It was another place where the remains of the convict past felt very strong. Much of the ground was strewn with old shells wedged into the sandy soil from the Aboriginals who had journeyed there for shellfish. I loved the Cape Barren Geese and was thrilled to see so many birds. Wild wombats also grazed fearlessly in the tussock grass later in the day.

Commissariat's Store

On our regular car trips before the arrival of mandatory seat belts, we children rolled around on the backseat unrestrained, particularly when we travelled over 'the Sideling.' There were numerous hair-pin corners for Dad to negotiate and he had no thought of us as he whizzed along. It was heaps of fun. We'd deliberately let go of the seat so that we could pile on top of each other in a crazed heap, laughing hysterically.

I was frightened of cemeteries as a small girl and closed my eyes tight and turned away when we approached one on car journeys. As a toddler some kids terrified me with a scary song about deadybones that went, 'the worms crawl in and the worms crawl out...'

Many kids were passive smokers in their parents' cars. In vogue was the pipe - a hip bachelor accessory. A young man could look distinguished with this useful prop. My dad, forever the dandy, pipe smoked with gusto, while my mother was an occasional cigarette smoker. Imagine travelling long distance with windows wound up against the chilly Tasmanian weather, with parents smoking...

Trips to Hobart to see Mum's parents were a huge effort for Dad, who would grumble about driving such a long way - about two and a half hours on the old Midlands Highway. He'd get the car serviced and the tyres checked. Sandwiches would be packed for a picnic halfway as we were all so tired from the long journey that we'd have to stop to revive! My sister was not a good traveller. Perhaps it was that she loved to read on a long journey. We often stopped at Oatlands for a strawberry milkshake. Any wonder that before we got to Ross, Dad stopped the car in a hurry so Roslyn could be sick by the road side.

We visited many places in Tasmania with our adventurous parents. Sometimes rather than go up the Midlands Highway, we would drive up the east coast of Tasmania, certainly a longer route but one with lots of interesting and pretty spots to visit. Mum and Dad liked to stop at Coles Bay. My artistic Mum said the East Coast of Tasmania felt almost Mediterranean; it was sunnier with less frosts in Winter and the light was softer somehow.

At Coles Bay we camped or stayed at The Chateau, family friendly motel units where Frecinet Lodge is now. We visited my friend Keeva, who had a shack there, so we, Keeva and her brothers all ran about together, exploring and swimming, boating and fishing. Marcus was in heaven! Dad and Mum bought fresh scallops at the Fisheries and we all went for a big day walk over the Hazards, to Wineglass Bay. Keeva's Dad had even made an F Troop tower in her backyard for us to play on!

Seal Rock

The fibro shack at St Helens where we stayed had an old bath tub set outside. We had to fill it up with the hose and set a fire going underneath to warm up the water. What a heap of fun it was to have a bath at night under the stars with the smell of wood smoke in the air! Dad and Marcus went fishing off the beach the next day and we tried crayfish for the first time. Yum! I loved all the fishing-boats tied up at the jetty and later did a painting of them.

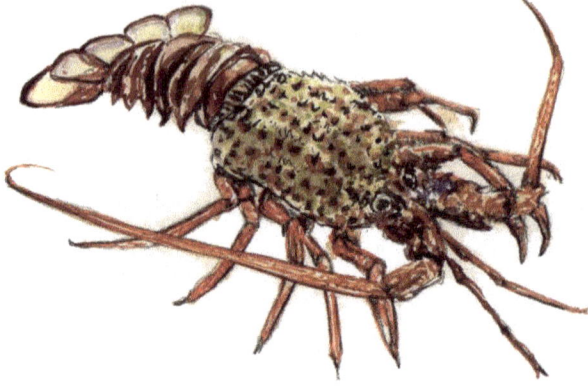

At Bicheno we stayed at the Silver Sands Hotel. It had a pool in the middle of the units and we all enjoyed swimming there. Marcus and I fished off the jetty at the Gulch and we were thrilled to see fish swimming below us on our Glass Bottom Boat trip as we floated around Governor Island.

We climbed up to Whaler's Lookout and saw a huge Sea Eagle glide by. In the evening we went to the rookeries to see the fairy penguins.

Camping at Bridport was a tradition with my father's family and friends. Just before Christmas every year, the Goftons, Wheatleys, Gerkeys, Robinsons, Browns and Turners would camp above Eastman's Beach. They set up an old greyed rectangular canvas tents over picnic tables. A floor covering was made from hessian sacking sewn together with a bag needle. With no running water, everyone filled up buckets of tap water taken from the Brid River. It needed to stand overnight to let the black sediment drop to the bottom. Old tick mattresses served for sleeping. We all washed in a bucket or went to the Bridport Hotel for a hand-basin wash. There were about forty kids between the families. By the time Marcus was born, Mum decided that with three children under six, with one rather sick (me), it was too much in such primitive conditions. The next year we stayed in a garage with bunks. My mother bought a block at Bridport high up on Granite Rise and we had our shack built. I can just remember toddling along behind a train of kids, threading our way through the nearby fair-ground, all lit up with lots of coloured lights in the evening.

Along with the joys of sun and sea, Bridport was all about fishing trips for our dads. Dad's uncle Alan Wheatley would row a little boat out at twilight with one end of a net that stretched back to waiting people on the beach. We kids stood in the shallows, splashing about to frighten fish into the net, which was then pulled into shore. Long before the enormous drift nets of today, small purseining nets were used to collect fish in this way. There would be so many caught - mostly flat-head, pike and cod. Once a little boy my age stepped on a stingray in the shallows and had to be rushed to hospital in Scottsdale. A mass gutting and de-heading occurred with seagulls screaming and diving. With such enormous quantities of fish and many hungry families to feed, fires were lit on the beach and big frypans set upon them to cook the catch.

The dads wrapped up the extra fish in newspapers and delivered them to mates, on the way to the pub to buy a keg of beer. Everyone settled in for a traditional Christmas beach barbeque, sometimes with lightning shows out to sea in Bass Strait - there was even an eclipse one year!

Mermaid's Pool is a natural small beach between the rocks. When the tide is in it is just like a real swimming pool and then it is deep enough for the bigger kids to take turns at jumping from the big granite boulders.

On the other side a flatter rock made a great spot for mums and toddlers to congregate. Whether the tide was in or out, there was always something to do and places to explore. a gang of kids would congregate on top of the big rock. For the more adventurous older kids and parents, it is quite possible to walk from Mermaid's Pool to Lades beach across the coastal granite platform.

A favourite trick of kids up on the big rock was to shout 'stingray!' down to those below in the water. My we hurried to get our legs up on paddle boards and lilos!

One year while the daddies were all fishing or boating, all the mums and children crossed the Brid River at low-tide. The aim was to walk right along the beach to the 'Cut.' The trek took us along past the big farms at Barnbougle and then to where the Little Forester River crossed the beach. We turned in there and walked up beside the river to the bridge over the road. The timing was right; in no time various fathers arrived to pick up the tired but happy mob. We found some lovely shells on the way that day.

I adored the beach and still do. We were so lucky to have a a clever Mummy who made our sunhats and pretty shirred swimsuits. We were in and out of the water so much so hats were only worn occasionally. By summer's end we were really tanned though never had serious sunburn. When our sunburn did peel, we thought it fascinating! We ran and swam, paddled and fossicked all day long and grew fit and strong.

When we were old enough, at low tide we would walk from Mermaid's Pool beach to Old Pier Beach. Other beaches we used to explore were named after families who had lived there for a long time. These were Mattingly's, Eastman's and Gofton's.

There were so many interesting shells to discover - cowries, volutes, painted pheasant shells, scallops, crab's nippers, shark eggs and sea urchins. The beach is no different today for children; it is a place of marvels - sand, sea, rock-pools and sand-dunes. All the beaches were safe for little children to wander along, and we did!

Dad adored Bridport and was at his happiest when out in his boat, named 'Rodima', after the first two letters of each of our names; Roslyn, Diana and Marcus. Dad and Mum built our boat down under the house at Trevallyn - I recall them steaming the planks over the kitchen kettle to curve them. The Perkins motor was troublesome, leaving us stranded a few times. It was replaced by a Mercury, which was much better. Often by seven in the morning, our family would be down at the ramp, piling into Rodima for a wonderful trip, some fishing and exploring.

We knew the 'couta' were running out in the bay because seabirds would be in a frenzy. Dad would say, 'hurry, hurry, we must go out now!' We trailed a long line with a huge hook behind the boat and immediately were pulling a huge long silvery fish into the boat. There were showers of scales flying off the fish as they landed. Sometimes we caught so many fish as did all the others fishing, that I felt quite sorry for the poor things thrashing around our legs on the bottom of the boat. I caught a big one on my line that nearly pulled me out of the boat until Dad came to my rescue and took over to bring the fish in. When we got back to shore and measured the couta, it was 3" 6' or 1 metre 15 cm. I wasn't much bigger myself and felt very proud.

Before the day got too hot, we'd head back to the ramp, hitch the boat to the trailer and buy some hot tank loaves and a billy of milk on the way home for a late breakfast. Often we were so hungry from our early start that the loaf of warm fragrant bread had holes in the middle of the loaf.

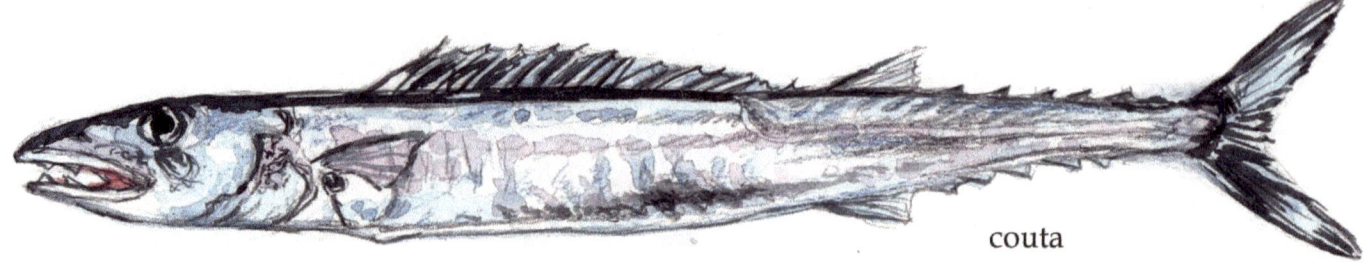

couta

We happily spent many weekends and holidays at Bridport which is less than an hour's drive from Launceston. Often we would leave straight after work on Fridays and have dinner at the shack. Marcus and I would often wander along to the Bridport jetty to sit and fish. Usually we could catch small black bream or sometimes a mullet.

Dad made Marcus and I a small shoe-boat dinghy to row about in. It was lots of fun. Marcus has had many boats since then.

On a cloudy day at Mermaid's Pool, us kids were surrounded by a school of couta. It might have been dangerous with all those sharp snapping teeth but it wasn't at all. A couple of parents watched, telling us not to move about too much and after ten magical minutes, the long silvery fish swam back out to sea.

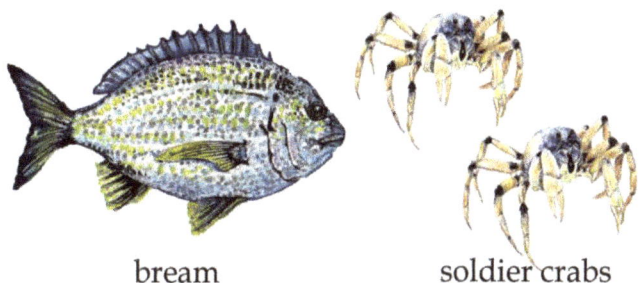

bream   soldier crabs

The granite rock platform from Mermaid's Pool to Lades beach grows natural orange lichen common to the Tassie's northeast and Flinder's Island. A test for the little kids was to jump over the gap between the two orange and grey boulders while older children leapt across with ease. A lovely walk can be taken from Mermaid's to Lades Beach on these rocks and there are some wonderfully deep, round rock-pools along the way.

Elephant Rock marks the junction between Eastman's and Gofton's Beach. It is a large granite boulder that deters tiny kids from climbing it as the first toehold is quite high up. When old enough we all felt quite a sense of achievement to get to the top. In the steep bank behind it, among the wattles and she-oaks there was a hexagonal wooden rotunda with a shingle roof for picnics and for bands to play in.

We built forts among the native black-boys. Home away from home with apples in a burlap sack and a mug for drinks.

The best sandcastles are near the sea with a trench to get the tide into your mote. Decorating with drippy sand is fun too.

Wonderful rockpools with green seastars to find, anenomes to poke, crabs to catch and periwinkles to collect.

'Mummy, we've found an octopus in a rock-pool.'
'It's a Blue Ringed Octopus, very dangerous!'
We let it wash away with the next wave.

In Summer, on sandy tracks it was easy to find pretty green and magenta Christmas beetles. It was fun to let them crawl on you with their prickly feet.

At the Brid River we'd collect grasshoppers to catch Rainbow Trout with. Marcus and Dad would fly fish from the bank while the girls looked for field mushrooms.

From the western end of Lades Beach at Bridport it was possible to walk across the sand dunes on Double Sandy Cape to St Alban's Bay. Occasionally another family, the Carruthers, would join us for this huge walk to explore Aboriginal middens in the shifting sands and fossick for shells after a well earned picnic lunch on the uninhabited beach.

Once Marcus kept loading Mum's cane basket with rocks and found a fabulous Aboriginal flint. I would roam the sand to feel the Aboriginal spirits among the middens in the dunes. Then it was back again on exhausted little legs - a good 6 to 10km walk and a great experience for everyone.

Just outside Bridport on the Scottsdale Road we could hire ponies then. Riding became a regular holiday pastime for my sister, brother and I. We often had friends come to stay at our shack, so naturally when my best friend Joyce came to stay; we spent every minute on our horses. We would walk the ponies through Bridport and along the lovely beaches, eventually arriving at Lades Beach. There was a fire trail behind the dunes to explore, and then down onto the sand we'd go, for a canter or a gallop in the shallows. What fun!

With thirsty ponies, we girls would ride up to our shack and tie up in the backyard, much to the horror of our cat Minny, who flew into a panic at the sight of such huge animals.

A few times we went to Mrs. Shipp's Riding School at Cuckoo, near Scottsdale. We'd take our clothes, pillows and sleeping bags, to sleep on camp beds in a couple of old wool sheds. After a country brekky, we'd muck out stalls, then groom and ride our ponies. Mrs. Shipp who ran the riding school was pretty easygoing - we had heaps of freedom, but there were rules such as how to correctly saddle our mounts. Some Shetland ponies are wily and hold their breaths when a saddle goes on their backs. My little brother Marcus would not have known this as he tightened up the girth straps. Once in the saddle, the inevitable happened - when the pony let out its breath, the saddle slid round and Marcus fell off the tail end. At least it wasn't too far to the ground.

The highlight of the camp was an all day trek through the bush to the top of Bomber's Hill. After a picnic lunch, we'd have an exhilarating gallop back downto the riding school. After dinner we were treated to a disco with enjoyable bush-band music held at a wool shed down the road. Terrific fun!

At two or three I was already fascinated by horses. There was a paddock behind Nanna's house at Talbot Road where horse riders would take their mounts over home grown jumps. When I was five I was climbing the fence to watch and dream. One day a girl came up to the fence to talk to me and wonder of wonders, she helped me crawl over the fence and onto her pony with her!

Most horse-mad children willingly do all the tasks assigned to care for horses: mucking out stalls, currying and grooming, cleaning tack and caring for hooves.

By late childhood we lived and breathed horses. Joyce luckily had her own pony bought for her. 'Chiefy,' was agisted at Michelle's Riding School at Riverside. We spent all our spare time there. Despite not having my own pony I rode regularly but I am sure I pestered my parents mercilessly for a horse. Riding gave me a peace and contentment that no other activity could match. This naturally led on to me studying horse history, anatomy, health, horse breeds, reading fiction and non fiction about horses, horsy art and even studying Gunsynd and the Melbourne Cup! An interest in art grew with the beloved subject and I found myself able to draw horses really well.

Liffey Falls was a popular family destination only an hour's drive from Launceston. It is one of many beautiful waterfalls in Tassie - and there are so many to choose from! Other than Liffy, our other favorites were Montezuma Falls and Russell Falls. There used to be an old iron ladder up the side of the falls that we climbed up. As a very small child I can remember how terrified I was crawling up the ladder because it was so wet and slippery. I'll never forget seeing my first leech at Liffy - and needless to say we took great care to never get a leech on us; we'd always tuck our pants into our socks and carry some salt or vinegar or matches.

Weekends often meant drives out into the country, sometimes along unsealed back-roads. Our Dad, like many other dads was always on the look-out for fallen trees to cut up for free firewood.

Often on country roads we'd see cows who'd gotten over the fences and were happily eating the verge grass, or at other times, whole herds of sheep or cows took over the road ahead as farmers transferred their stock to different paddocks or up to the milking shed.

Meanwhile Mum was interested in finding wild flowers and fossils so we found and learned to identify a number of native orchids - Greenhoods, Sun and Flying Duck orchids. We turned over all sorts of rocks to see if we could find agates or fossils. We might wander through paddocks and over stiles to find fresh mushrooms or blackberries for blackberry pie too. All this fossicking was such a pleasure for little kids.

During the first months of high school I made friends with a girl who was from Flinder's Island. When she went back for the February Long Weekend, I went to stay with her. She lived just out of Whitemark on a farm. The landscape seemed very similar to the 'mainland' of Tasmania, but rather windy from the Roaring Forties blowing over the island. We went kayaking around the bays and also walked some of the way up Strzlecki, the highest point on the island.
One evening we went mutton birding, or rather, the adults did, while we held hurricane lanterns and watched while people searched for the holes the birds had made for nesting. They reached in and pulled the chicks out, quickly breaking their necks. Very soon, the hunters had several dangling at their sides or hung over a stick to be carried to a shed for plucking and processing.
Another evening there was a bonfire. A wallaby had been killed and hung up nearby, where one of the men peeled off its hide like a sock and it was then roasted over the fire.

King Solomons Cave

We were all very excited to be going to visit Mole Creek caves. A short drive west of Deloraine and we were there! First we went to King Solomons Cave. Our guide took us from the bright sunlight into a strange and wondrous world. It seemed scary to be underground, yet so marvellous to see coloured stalacmites and columns in such profusion. Our guide told us there were over three hundred limestone caves in the area but only a few of those had magnificent decorations like these.
We visited Honeycomb Caves next - part of the Wet Cave reserve. I felt so small and held onto Mum's hand as there were no lights or pathways in this cave. It was very dark and slippery.
Last of all we visited Marakoopa Cave which had crystals, stalactites, stalagmites and… glow worms! There were two creeks running through it with pools of water and marvellous reflections. We were all amazed by the magical caves at Mole Creek.

Marakoopa Cave

One winter we stayed in the old fashioned bush hut at Cradle Mountain for a long weekend. We were lucky as there had been quite a cover of snow - Mum was able to show us how to ski a little. Two other families who were old friends of Mum - the Fords and the Carringtons came too, so there were another six children to share the fun of throwing snowballs and making snowmen. Of course we loved all the mountain possums and currawongs that visited us where we stayed.

When I was a small girl I would look at my little button nose in the mirror and believe that I was an Aborigine despite my red hair and pale skin. In the 60s, we were taught that our white forebears had killed off all the Tasmanian Aborigines. I felt a kind of collective shame about that. Our convict heritage, the loss of the Aboriginal native people and the extinction of the Tasmanian Tiger were part of a darker internal picture that we Tasmanian children grew into. As my mum and Uncle Henry were very interested in Aboriginal history and artefacts, Roslyn, Marcus and I knew Truganini's sad story, but strangely didn't know until later as adults that there were and are still Tasmanian Aborigines in Tasmania.

When news of the pristine wilderness at the Franklin River and Lake Pedder being tampered with by the Hydro Electric Commission (HEC) was aired on the TV news in the late 60s, I was immediately interested. My friend Joyce and I began to collect newspaper cuttings and talk about it with other children at school as our fledgling political interest was piqued. Having an older sister who talked to me about it, helped too. We had all been educated from an early age as to the positive attributes of the 'Hydro,' Tasmania's Hydro-Electric Commission. We visited dams as Sunday outings sometimes and the newsreels before films at the Princess Theatre were often stirring tales about the Hydo's benefit to the state. When it came to flooding such a beautiful wild lake with its pink quartzite beach, Tasmanians like my family disapproved; even though we had not been there, its destruction hit the collective nerve that held the Tassie Tiger, Tasmanian Aborigines and beleaguered convicts. That's how it seemed to me at ten or twelve years of age, though I knew too that others saw it as a benefit to the state.

My mum had been a member of the Hobart Walking Club for many years. My mum knew that since the 1950s, it had been understood that Lake Pedder National Park should be kept pristine for future generations. Debate and concern raged on through the 70s and 80s until the area was indeed flooded. A statue of Truganini's bust set at Lake Peddar before its flooding, expressed a concern that appealed to the inner sense of being Tasmanian, one where the beauty of our island touches our hearts, whether we are still young and small or much older and tall.

Truganini 1803 – 1876 'When we reflect on the beauty and dignity of Truganini, we must deplore the destruction of her people. Let us reflect on the beauty of this lake, dedicated to the memory of Truganini and her people and resolve to keep it unspoiled for the benefit of mankind.'

Acknowledgements

When I was a small girl just learning to write, my mother encouraged me to make little books and illustrate my imaginative tales. To be able to conjure stories with pictures became a mainstay of my life, both personally and professionally. It is a gift to give children time - time to write, dream and draw, even in this age where we are all so busy and saturated with media and computer based opportunities.

The idea to write this book grew from my mother, a professional illustrator and artist herself. She produced three books, 'A Small Girl's Hobart - 1936- 1946, Volume 1 & 2 and 'Fashion and Design,' before her death in 2014. Mum suggested I create a similar book about growing up in the 1960s. The opportunity to share the family's collective memories with her has been an invaluably rich experience. Mum shed light on many of my dimly remembered memories and helped with points of illustration - her knowledge and accuracy supersedes mine. A huge thank you!

Through this book's creation I have revisited forgotten friendships, places and connections. My best childhood friend Joyce Ivers and I relived a rich vein of memory together and reformed our friendship after 40 years apart. An old school chum Keeva Leighton (Gray) has been an invaluable help with points of memory and images - many thanks.

My partner Jason Julian and my children James, Justin and Jemma have kindly accepted my preoccupation with my past for a time to create my own version of family history. Thank you for your support, love and encouragement. Both my sister Roslyn and brother Marcus have been enthusiastic about this project and offered up their memories, insights and suggestions - what lovely siblings both then and now.

Many Tasmanians have done special research or given reference and information to me that I wish to thank personally:

Alex Van Der Hek, Bridport Visitor Centre, Bridport jetty- Judy Barnett, Gourlays sweet shop - Michael Wood, Jeff Jenkins - Bridport history, Justin Julian - Queen Elizabeth 11 illustration, Mary Reynolds - Merrington illustration, Midlands Council, Tasmania -Sharon Rawnsley - topiary, Queen Victoria Museum and Art Gallery - Ross Smith, Spotless Cleaning Company - Bonami, Tasmanian Fire Museum - Terry Gill & Roger McNeice, Tata Global Beverages - Gail McLardie - Tynee Tips tea cards, Trevallyn Primary School - Nicki Cassidy, Veronica Timperon (Clarke) - old photos, Kraft Foods Australia - Cadbury, Launceston City Council, Tasmania - Debbie Pickett and Chris Moore. Lorraine Green - Northern Midlands Council, Sandra Grining – West Coast Heritage Centre, Paul Flood – Tasmanian Parks & Wildlife, Lennie Jack – Opossum Bay, Rona Hollingsworth – Tasmanian Maritime Museum, Jacqui Ward – Hobart Museum & Art Gallery, Sweets n Treats – Richmond, Alan Fletcher – Tassie Birds, Anthony Quin - Silver Sands Hotel

A Small Girl's 1960s Launceston
2nd Edition

Design, text & illustrations
© Copyright Diana Reynolds 2016

The moral right of the author has been asserted.

All rights reserved. No part of this book can be reproduced or transmitted by any person or entity, including internet search engines or retailers, in any form or by any means, electronic or mechanical, including photocopying (except under the statutory exceptions provisions of the Australian Copyright Act 1968), recording, scanning or by any information storage and retrieval system without the prior written permission of Diana Reynolds.

Printed by Ingram Spark/Lightning Source Australia

ISBN: 978-0-9942485-7-2
Catalogue Listing National Library of Australia

For more information & sales please contact:

gallerydiana@gmail.com
Diana Reynolds +61 2 8090 8878

'You bury your childhood here and there. It waits for you, all your life, to come back and dig it up.'

Anthony Doerr

www.ingramcontent.com/pod-product-compliance
Lightning Source LLC
Chambersburg PA
CBHW061934290426
44113CB00024B/2904